"GE...

Notes from the Lord

By
Dorothy Sannes

Published By
James and Dorothy Sannes
for.hisglory@verizon.net

The poems in this book was inspired and given to me by the Lord. I was encouraged by my Pastor's wife, Vivian Cunningham, to begin to write down what the Lord was giving me. I wish to thank Fran and Bill Cook, Dave and Sally White and Sharon Ransom for their prayers and words of encouragement. A thanks to Fran for reading them for me. I want to thank A'lyce Baldarelli for giving me the idea for the Title of "Note from the Lord" instead of just "NOTES"
I want to thank my husband for believing in me.

LOVE & GRACE

I have a psalm that was
Given me full of love
& Grace, My heart drinks
From each line the grace
So rich and fine
My Lord redeemer friend
Of mine,
He said He'd keep me safe
He'd hide me in His arms,
Oh His love and grace a psalm
Was given me. I read, I cry,
And then I pray I sing
And dance and then I say,
My heart grows stronger
With each phase
Oh Lord I give You praise,
To me a psalm was given.

#1 7-26-98

COME AND DANCE

Come and dance with me
I have the steps
I have the music too,
Reach out your hand
I'll guide you through
Come dance with me,
Come dance with me
I'll show you more and more,
Around you now to others
Say, Come join the dance
Yes dance with me.

Oh Lord I want to stay
Close by your side, and
Learn yes learn the steps
And hear the music in my
Heart that's there You
Put I know,
I'll dance with you,
I'll dance with you,
Oh Lord don't let me go.

#2 7-26-98

YOUR STRENGTH NOT MINE

I have no strength of my own
In you oh Lord there is,
Beside me walk and hold
My hand, before me
Clear my path,
Your strength within me Lord
Is only how I stand.

I have no strength of my own
I feel you all around
Touching me, telling me,
I'm not on my own,
I love to hear You whisper
Gentle in my ear,
Lovingly You say to me,
I am Yours alone.

#3 7-26-98

TALK

Your life grows strong
Within me Lord, each
Day I am with You,
I cannot take another step
Until I talk to you.

So listen Lord as I pray,
To You, I want to say
Lord keep me close to You
And in your presence near,
And help me do the things
That You say do.
So grow within me Lord
And make me strong within,
So that through the days
Your spirit, in me, stays.

#4 7-26-98

HIS GREATNESS

Above us and about us
Are the works of His hands,
It's only for us to see!
Open your eyes and look around
His beauty to behold
He made it all, that He did,
He's mighty yet He's gentle,
Mountains high and seas that roar,
The lion that makes you tremble,
He's in control of everything,
Open your eyes and see
The beauty of the Masters hand
The artist of the soul.

#5 7-26-98

THE DAYS DAWN

Each day I rise
I need You more
You grow within me Lord
Your words of love
Reach down to me
Your blessings I receive.

#6 7-26-98

DANCE WITH ME

Open your heart and
Come dance with Me,
Reach out your hand and I'll
Teach you how,
Come dance with Me
I have the music
Come dance with Me
Step after step
You can learn from Me,
Come dance with Me
I am your partner
Now dance with Me.

#7 7-26-98

LOVE GIVEN

At night it comes to me
The greatness of Your love
Beyond my understanding,
You have given me
A promise of that love,
Line after line
You say to me,
I love you child,
Remember so you'll know.

#8   7-26-98

IN THE NIGHT

You give me poems within
The night to bless and
Strengthen me,
The words are left there
In the night
I cannot say aloud how
Can I say them in the light?
To Him they are within,
I keep them there for now
I can't remember yet!
The poems given in the night
For there is just a glimpse
Of what is said,
In the middle of the night.

#9   7-26-98

REMINDER OF THE DANCE

You keep saying dance with
Me that's for sure I know
My feet they seem to
Stumble, You say to
Hold Your Hand
You'll guide me there,
I know the music's in
My heart and You have
Said lets dance!
I have to listen closely,
So that I can hear,
The beauty You've created
Deep within me there.
I will learn the steps
That You have set before me,
As You keep reminding me
To dance with You,
I'm here.

#10 7-26-98

A BRIDGE TO CROSS

A bridge to cross
Sometimes too far,
I think I cannot make it
Often fog and dark clouds
Loom above me as I go,
In faith I take a step
To walk across with my
Hand in Yours, I have to
Hold on Tightly so I will
Not slip,
I have to walk it straight
Across, there are no twists
Or turns a bridge, the
Path is set before me,
That is what I've learned.

#11 8-2-98

YELLOW ROSE

A rose I hold here in
My hand,
The color it is yellow,
I reach out for the
Memories it held dear
To me,
My heart cries out
No more! The
Yellow rose for me,

Written for my friend
#12 8-2-98 Lillian

A WALL OF BRICKS

A Wall of bricks I built
My self to stand behind
And hide,
Each day You take a brick
Off, to tear it down for me,
You don't want me hiding,
Down behind the wall,
I just keep on ducking
Lower and lower as it goes,
As the wall gets shorter
I see what I must do,
To stand up tall and
Trust You Lord
That Your word is true.

#13 8-4-98

THE VASE

The gems of many colors
They are being poured
Into a cut glass vessel,
They are things of beauty
I really can't explain
They each represent
a gift from God
To share with one another,
To give to those
Who are in need
My sister and my brother.
The vase sits there
For all to see
The gems they all do
Gleamier, they shine
Within me Lord
Others there to see,
Take a gem and share it now
The Lord has said to me.

#14   8-5-98

THE FENCE

The fence I walk
I love you Lord
I jump from side to side
On one side then the other,
The word I read
It's in my heart,
I do not understand
Just why I can't get
Close to you
To you I pray each day.
The fence I've walked
Unsteady as I go, this
Is where I need you Lord
To show me how to trust,
And listen to Your word!
Which side to walk,
And in my heart I'll know.

#15   8-5-98

THE MEADOW

There is a meadow deep
Within growing in my heart,
The Lord has put sweet
Flowers there to blossom
One by one,
I walk along the pathway
Directed by His hand,
He shows Me growth within
My life as the flowers bloom,
The beauty deep within me
Comes from Him and Him alone.
This path smells sweet
And I can walk on through
This time of my life,
For now I see what
He's put there
A meadow in my heart.

#16   8-5-98

EAGLES' HEIGHTS

See the beauty all around
As the eagle soars,
There is great strength
In his wings
As he opens wide,
To uplift us and to glide
Along the wind stream high,
To take us up to new heights
And to worship more,
In his presence we can see
On eagles' wings
Struggle there's no more.

#17   8-6-98

A PATH

A path of stones are set
Before you the words are
Written there just how
To take each step by step
Faith, trust, hope and
Believe the next stone
Says discernment
So read before you walk
And trust the Lord
He knows your path for
He has walked before you..

#18   8-6-98

MY DISCIPLE

You are my disciple
That, I've said before,
Go among my people
Teach them about my word,
Love and peace and grace
I give to them who will
believe,
In Me the way you see
There is no other.
My yoke is easy
My way is right
To all who enter here,
So choose your path
And teach My word
For you are My disciple.

#19   8-6-98

A MIRACLE

The making of a miracle
Is for us to see
It is for the asking
Reach out and believe,
He is there awaiting
Wanting us to receive
All that He has for us
In His word He speaks, yes
It's there for the asking
a miracle you see.

#20   8-9-98

MY FRIEND

My friend you are!
He says to me
I cannot tell a lie,
He walks beside me
Day by day my hand
He hold's on tight,
So that I will know
That fast or slow
With my friend I'm walking.

#21   8-10-98

THE DANCE

I've danced the dance
I've walked the walk
You've twirled me all
Around the dance I know
You've guided me
With your mighty hand
You've placed me where
You wanted me
Here on solid ground.

#22   8-10-98

YOUR WORDS

The spirit deep within
Me longs to hear
Him say,
You are my child
I love you so
I'm with you today,
Tomorrow and the next
Day then, the next
Day and always.

You've blessed me Lord
With words to say
How much you are around,
Your grace is great
And love to me
Is greatly to be found.

The words you say
I only have to look within
Me Lord Your spirit's
Resting there.

#23   8-10-98

MY ROCK

You are my Rock
On which I stand, it's
Written in your word,
The Rock is firm
It does not move
Each step I take is true,
Your word says ask of Me
And I'll be there to
Comfort when in trouble,
Just take a step in faith
I'll walk with you
In Him there is no other.

#24   8-10-98

ANGLES

He said He'd send His
Angles to watch and
Guard orr me,
With their hand they
Steady me they'll shut a
Lions' mouth, they even
Stirred the waters at
Bethesda's pool for
Some healings there,
They even walk beside me
Protecting with great care.

#25   8-11-98

LITTLE ANGLE

You are my little angle
Sent from up above
Sent down here to bless me
With your presence near,
Thou you're just a
Little girl
Grown but not just yet
You have given Gods
True love
Each day you're alive,
You grow in grace
And beauty
In that I now see,
You are my little angle
Living here with me.

Written for my friend Pat
#26   8-10-98

MY SHEPHERD

Oh Lord You are my shepherd
In You I shall not want
Is what You say to me,
I'll walk on paths of
Righteousness, You leading
All the way, we rest
Beside still waters
Down in the meadow cool,
You walk me through the
Valley dark, You guide
Me all the way,
You protect me from my
Enemies in the midst
Of noonday meal,
Your goodness overflows me
With your blessings here
You have given new
Life to me Lord
With heavens care.

#27 8-11-98

SWEET PEACE

Lord You are my comfort
In You I put my trust
For me there is no other,
Who gives sweet peace
And strength to me
When I think
I am in trouble,

So help me Lord
To first thank You at
The beginning of the day,
So we start together
And my peace will stay.

#28   8-11-98

OUR ANGLES

We have three little angles
Gifts from God we know,
Their names are
A.J., Paul & Joshua
Oh Lord we love them so,
His spirit's deep within
Their hearts so to help
Them grow, yes!
From the start they've
Showed us love as pure as
Pure can be because
It's unconditionally,
That's the love that
You've put there,
Into our three little angles.

#29   8-12-98

SONG OF PRAISE

Your song I sing is deep
Within waiting to get out,
I sing the song within my
Heart a melody of light,
You bring sweet peace and
Rest to me in the middle
Of the night,

A song of praise I sing
To You, a song that
Says deliverance a song
Of great delight,
I sing a song I sing to
You for it's like no other,
Sing it now and sing it
Loud, just sing it
With all your might.

#30   8-12-98

HIS FIRE

Oh lord You filled my heart
You've put a fire in me,
Spread the flames around
So others they might see,
The mighty works of
Your hands, the fire
You put in me,
I must pursue Him more
And more to flame
That fire from thee,
Spend more time
Declare his word,
Refine that fire in me.

#31   8-13-98

YOU CALL ME FRIEND

Knowing the life that you
Laid down, the love
You gave to me,
You have chosen and
Called on me and
You have called me friend,
You promised to protect
Me yes,
Your life You gave for me,
I have chosen to believe,
That to the end
You'll stay my friend as
Long as I walk with thee.

#32   8-13-98

ROSEBUD

Her life is like a rosebud
Awaiting her turn to bloom,
The spirits deep within her
Growing strong we know,
Waiting for the right time
For Him to say lets go;
The fragrant it's so sweet
To smell it is the Holy
Spirit, she's opened up to
Let it flow her life's
Began to show the fragrance
Of that rosebud, the Rose,
It's fully grown.

#33   8-14-98

GENTLE MOMENTS

Gentle moments come
With just a breeze,
A breath of God
That comes to please,
The gentle heart
That will receive the
Words He has to speak,
His voice it can be soft
Within the gentle moments
Of sweet peace.

#34   8-15-98

CROSSROADS

You said I'm at a crossroad,
A decision I'll have to make
Which path You've set before
Me, I only have to choose,
It's there I stand to
Check it out, to see
What I can see, and look
At all my choices, Your
Word I read Your path
I'll take, for there
You'll walk beside me.

#35   8-15-98

NEW STRENGTH

New strength will grow as
He emerges out of deep
Within, the Lord stirs up
His spirit as He is
Revealed the sweetness of
His love for me and
Gives me oh such peace,
Each day he comes to give me
More and more to say about
His love and gentleness
And kindness oh so sweet,
And oh I know, You won't
Let go so please don't
Pass me by,
Your words say dance
With Me
I say I'm here!
Beneath the summer sky.

#36   8-15-98

YOUR VESSEL

Oh Lord I am Your vessel
Fill me to the top
For my heart desires of
You all that You can give,
The blessings of Your sweet
Peace and Your grace poured
In mix it all together
What You say I'll do,
Just what You have created
Lord I pray it's You.

#37   8-15-98

A MANTEL

You've given me a mantel
You said it would not hurt
Because You have created
And given it to me,
You said it's Your
Anointing, I'll ware it
Like a coat, the richness
Of Your words in me is in
My innermost being, there
Will be a transformation
Taking place in me, and the
Anointing of God will stay,
The time will show He'll
Let me know, it'll come
From my innermost being.

#38   8-15-98

OUR HEARTS

Our hearts will join
In one accord as we begin
To gather, His spirit
Pours as there is more,
Into our hearts He'd rather
Give to us just what we need
Because there is no other.
Each heart that joins
And there is more each one
Is just as beautiful,
Right from the start
He has our heart and
There He is right with us,
For on us there
He pours with care
On us the Holy Spirit.

#39   8-17-98

OUR HERO

My hero, Jesus Christ
He came from purity,
He grew and knew
And at the age of twelve,
The word He spoke
And that's no joke about
His heavenly father,
They left Him there
But did not know
That He was left behind
They did go back
Three days did pass, they
Found Him in the temple,
His mother knew and
Pondered through
But kept it to herself,
His wisdom grew
And that she knew
Jesus is our hero.

#40   8-17-98

JUST ASK

The Lord He knows just what
I need even when I don't
With every task
He says just ask, for
He is right there listening,
He knows our heart
Right from the start, and
That is why He's saying,
There's treasures there
He's put with care,
To help us with our healing,
He said just ask
His love will last,
The Lord He is our keeper.

#41 8-19-98

RENEWED ASSURANCE

The storms once raged
About me, I thought
I could not cope,
Then with Your arms
You sheltered me, and
Brought to me new hope,
You brought me through
The hardships and gave
Me peace within, and
Though I knew no answers,
At times it seemed so hard,
I only had to trust You
On You I could depend.
You brought renewing to
My soul and sweet
Assurance too!
I look back now, and
I can see Your hand has
Been on me, and
Now the sweet assurance
Is sweeping over me, and
I can see new meaning
In my life with thee!

#42   8-20-98

SOARING

You've poured into my
Spirit all that gives me
Strength, my heart, it wants
To soar like the mighty
Ocean that roars, with
The beauty of Your majesty
I can shine like never
Before, the strength
That gives the light,
The gift that'll help
Me soar, it's there
Because You filled me Lord,
With Your mighty power.

#43   8-24-98

YOUR ROSES

In me there grows a garden
The beauty is complete,
The fragrance oh so sweet,
It's there the roses grow
Lord, the colors they are
From You, yellow is for
The crown You wore
There upon Your head,
Red is for the blood
You shed,
Purple is for the robe
You wore down the path
That lay ahead,
White is for the
Life You gave
For our sins that day.
And now I stand here
Looking at the beauty
You've placed within,
You sent Your Holy Spirit
For the fragrance of
Your life in me is
here to stay.

#44   8-24-98

THE LORDS MAN

There was a ministering soul
The Lord did make him whole,
His life did show
Just what was known
Within him where he walked,
His words they grew
And he did show
As he began to talk,
And as he spoke
Each one would know, that,
He was filled
With the Holy Spirit.
As each day past
His words would last
For it was the Holy spirit.
The wolves came by
And they did try,
To nip him from behind,
But the Lord said NO
You'll have to go,
For this man he is mine.

#45   8-24-98

HIS SONG

To sing the words of Your
Sweet peace with gentleness
Of voice, to sing out loud
The mighty message that
You have said's
Your choice, to sing
The songs of melody and
Sing them from the heart,
Sing aloud with gladness
And sing among the nations,
Sing aloud with power
Sing aloud thy mercy's,
Unto Thee O Lord
For You are our salvation.
Sing a song to the Lord
Above a song right from the
Heavens, sing it there
Sing it every where, a
New song before the throne
With a heart of love.

#46   8-24-98

WALK WITH JESUS

I walk and talk with Jesus
These pages they do tell,
To me He gives assurance
Of how His love's so sweet,
My needs He's sure to meet.
I walk and talk with Jesus
My life's began to show,
New strength I have
To walk on through
Life's trials that, I know,
You've held my hand
And called me friend
And gave to me new hope,
That where I am, that,
I am not alone.

#47   8-24-98

WALK ON THROUGH

Walk on through
The Lords with you,
With His mighty power,
To see you through
He'll walk with you,
He'll give you strength
At this time and hour.
Just take your stand
Go through the land
Proclaiming Jesus words,
With His mighty power
He'll see you through
He'll walk with you
At this time and hour.
So walk on through
Yes, walk on through,
His word is oh so true,
He'll stay with you
His power too
For He shall walk with you,
At this time and hour.

#48   8-24-98

A BOY NAMED DAVID

There was a boy named David
He had three brothers
Follow Saul, and though
He was a shepherd
They didn't consider him
At all until one day
The giant came,
And David had the call
It came from God you see,
And David knew
The giant had to fall,
Five stones were laid
There on the ground
That David had to use,
He picked them up into
His pouch they went, then
Walked up to the giant
Where he knew he was sent
Took out a stone and aimed
It high, right from his
Sling did fly the stone did
Hit right on his head, the
Giant he did fall as he lay
There they did declare the
Giant he was dead. So
David grew and others knew
That he was Gods own man.

#49   8-24-98

THE WORD

Our God He is the Word
That's what my Bible says,
He started from the
Beginning He'll go
Until the end, He made
The world and everything,
The darkness and the
Light, He made a man in His
Own image, He loved us
From the start, but things
They changed when Adam
Sinned and God He knew just
What to do, that He would
Send His Son, to come to
Earth and live with man
Though sinless as He was,
He gave His life upon the
Cross for that was Gods
Own plan, to redeem us all
Through Christ His Son
So we can be with Him

#50   8-25-98

FAITH

We have real assurance
Through faith if we
Believe in Jesus Christ
The Son of God, eternal
Life is what we'll have
A gift you see we will
receive.
Tis joy to know that
Christ He died and gave
His life for you and me,
So we, if we believe
The gift of grace,
It's free you see to
Everyone who will receive.
So walk by faith through
Grace with the one who set
You free,
It's faith to faith
In righteousness of God
That's what He says to do,
A walk for me
A walk for you.

#51   8-30-98

YOUR MUSIC

The beat of the music
That You've set for me,
Is a beat that I can handle
But not without You Lord,
Sometimes it's fast
And sometimes it's slow,
But it's never one that
I cannot do,
You've set out the music
On the pages there
So clear,
I only have to read,
And keep it, the beat!
Oh dear!
It's in my heart Lord,
You've put the beat in me!

#52   8-30-98

GIVING YOU MY SONG

My life I give to you Oh
Lord to use in song and
Praise, my voice is
Yours to use to others
That they might
Hear Your message Lord,
Through singing songs of
You to sing those songs
Of love and about Your
Saving grace, to sing about
The things You've done,
About the cross and
Resurrection and about
You coming again, but
I cannot song these songs
Without You Lord
So I shall ask of you, to
Touch me Lord with
Your anointing so
I can sing for You.

#53   8-30-98

YOUR WORDS

I bring the words
That You have Lord,
The words You say to me,
The words that say
I love you, the words
That say believe, the words
Of Your deliverance, there
Are words of grace and
There are words of peace,
It's only for us to follow
The direction of Your path,
For it's there You laid it
Out for us there in the
Bible it is plain,
Your are the light
That lights the way,
It's there You say to walk.
Your words they tell about
Your comfort and Your
Strength, so this path
That You say walk
Is all in trusting You
With all our lives
In all we ever do.

#54 8-30-98

JOHN THE APOSTLE

John the Apostle, chosen by Jesus
One of the twelve he was, Peter
And John were companions a beloved
Disciple was he, the twelve who were
Chosen and told to go forth James
And John were sons of Zebedee, the
Lord said go preach let them all
Know that the kingdom of God
Is at hand.
Now Jesus He knew His time draweth
Near and He had instructions for
All, to Gethsemane, He went heavy
Of heart, He wanted His disciples
To pray, Peter, James
And John He took there while He
Fell on His face and prayed, then,
There He found the twelve were
Asleep and said, can't you watch
With Me just one hour?
There at the cross Jesus said from
His heart, John would you watch
And care for my mother?
For Jesus He knew that John
Had His heart and trustworthy
He knew that John was.
For John his last days he spent
There at Ephesus preaching and
Teaching about Jesus,
It was there he did write
The Gospel of John and of the
Miracles of Jesus his friend.

#55   9-1-98

YOU ARE THE LORD

You said You were my healer
Lord, You'd heal the hurts
Way from the past,
You are the Lord who
Said He'd provide for me
And give me just
What I needed, You said
To trust You and believe,
You said to give
From my own heart for
Unto me it would be given,
Yes, that I would then
Receive. Oh, but not
Just a little,
You'd press it down
And run it over this is
That what you have spoken,
Because the love
You have for me, that love
It's freely given, so
I am to give and I will see,
Just what You have for me.

#56   9-1-98

THE BEAUTY IN THE FLOWERS

Lord I see You in the flowers
It's there You help them grow,
It begins with a seed and
Just a little water, they
Sprout up with such beauty
And grow up oh so strong,
Then at the right moment
Their picked and put out on
Display for everyone to see.
For the flowers are our lives
The seed in us is You Lord,
We are given living water
To help us grow strong and
Beautiful, then in Your
Own time Lord You will
Choose us for display, and
You will use us Lord for
Your glory, for the beauty
There within us is the beauty
Of You Lord.
Lord the flowers there I see
You in me Lord, You are there,
Lord I'll do what You ask of me
I'll do what You say Lord.

#57 9-9-98

YOUR SERVANT

Oh Lord I am Your servant
To You I do belong,
I give to You my heart
My spirit and my soul,
So You can use me Lord
To speak to those
Who are in need
And others You can bring,
Into Your Kingdom Lord
So that they too might
Be freed.
Because I belong to You Lord
In Your presence I will sing
About Your love and saving
Grace and of the power
Deep within,
For it's there where
You are Lord,
Our hearts to You we bring.

#58   9-10-98

GET READY

Get your hearts ready
That's what He says to do,
The times drawing close, and
He really wants me and you
To keep our hearts strong and
Steady because we are His
Bride, a wedding is being
Prepared for us to attend,
The Lord He will meet us
When the trumpet says to
Ascend, that's why He keeps
Saying keep ready your
Hearts, we must keep our
Lights lit through our
Daily walk, for we know not
The hour that when the Lord
Will return, it's the signs
Of the time that shows it
Will be soon,
He's coming back with love
And He's coming with
Great power.

#59   9-14-98

THE CROSS

Upon the cross our Lord He
Died, with a crown of thorns
There on His head. He was
Beaten and pierced there in
His side, there He gave His life
For love on Him He took the
Sins for all, there on the cross
He hung between two thieves who
One did call "Oh Lord" forgive
This sinner here today, the
Lord said yes!
In paradise you will be with Me,
Then when the time it came He
Asked the Father to take the cup
From Him, the earth shook and
The heavens roared there the
Day death came to our Lord
Then from the cross they took
Him down, into a borrowed tomb
They laid Him there, three days
Then there did pass before the
Stone was rolled away by an
Angle there that day, and the
Lord He did arise then to
Those awaiting He did say here
On earth I cannot stay
To My Father I must go
But with My love I will send
The Holy Spirit here to you
To stay until the end.

#60   9-15-98

YOU ARE MY GOD

I'm still before You now
Speak to me I'm ready,
My heart is open to
Receive, Your presence to
Keep me walking steady,
For in you Oh God
I do believe that alone
You are my God and
You will be exalted,
The presence of Your peace
Has put gladness in my
Heart,
You are my refuge and my
Strength,
Oh God You saved me
From the start,
The Lord He is my salvation
In Him I put my trust.

#61   9-17-98

WORSHIP

The Lord calls us to worship
In fullness of our hearts,
He's asking us to worship
With all our power and might,
To stand beneath His mighty
Wings, and trust Him from
The start, for in trusting
Him our burdens light
For He's our burden bearer,
So we can sing to Him
Sweet melody that comes
Right from our hearts.
Our worship comes through
Our singing, it comes when
We're in prayer, it comes
Right from our hearts,
Now worship all you saints
Worship and sing praise,
For this day the Lord will
Say stand strong, believe,
He hears you when you pray,

#62   9-27-98

ALONG THE SHORE

Come walk with Me along the shore
And listen to the waves, the mighty
Ocean roar, they come in strong
Sometimes landing hard, then again
With just a breeze landing with
Such ease, the sand it changes
With each wave drawing in
And flowing out saying look at me
How I behave, I am here and
Then I'm gone, but yet my waves
Go on and on. The Lord says,
Come and walk with me along the
Shore take My hand and I'll
Show you more, the waves they
Are like the trials in our lives
Sometimes they are strong and
Mighty others come in like a
Breeze but yet they are there for
Us to see, knowing not for how
Long only that, like the sand
It's smooth and clean when the
Wave is gone, so you see, our
Trials my come and they may go
But as long as we walk along the
Shore holding on to the masters
Hand the trials of life will be
Like the sand washed
Away with each passing wave.

#63   10-5-98

GO TO HIM

Don't stay long in your
Frustration to the Father
You must go in the word
He will show how to walk
By faith alone, and your
Life will be full of grace
And possibility, for the
Lord can put there in
Your life peace and love
And fulfill your needs, so
Go to Him as soon as you
Can see frustration
Trying to overtake thee.

#64   10-5-98

SOARING LIKE THE EAGLE

Although I walk here on
The ground my spirit wants
To soar, I want to soar
Like eagles up to the
Mountain heights way beyond
The things that seem to hold
Me down, flying high on
Eagles wings trusting
You there Lord
To carry me to new heights
So that I can see as I
Rest there on the mountain
Top I can see what's there
For me, I soar on wings of
Eagles up to the mountain
Heights, Oh Lord You've
Lifted me, the things I
Once held tight I now release
To Thee, so as like eagles
I can soar for me, the
Fear there is no more.

#65   10-8-98

MY LOVE

I have a love a love
That You set forth,
It's here within me Lord
It's special in it's part
That love within my heart,
You've helped it grow
And then mature that love
Within my heart,
You've helped me know
And know for sure though
Many years have passed,
That the love I have for
Him that through those
Years my love is strictly
Just for Jim.

#66   10-8-98

THE FIRE

I stand here in Your presence
Lord receiving what You
Have for me,
I see the fire all around
I feel it burning in my heart,
The fire, the burning,
The sounds, the fire of the
Holy Spirit is burning the
Dross away, so Your presence
Here can stay, the sounds
Are of the singing the singing
Of all the saints, Your glory
Lord is shining through
When the dross is burned away.
I stand here in Your presence
Lord waiting for Your command
Waiting to hear where You say
Go to go and make my stand,
To dance with Holy reverence
Dance before Your thrown,
To sing of the one true God
The one who gives us peace,
To the one who gave us life,
And the one who sends His fire
To burn away the dross, so
That through Him and Him alone
We will be His own.

#67 10-27-98

FLYING HIGH

We fly like eagles Lord
In Your Spirit high,
We soar around and around
In worship without a sigh,
We've left our earthly
Troubles for You to care for
Lord, our hearts are in
Your presence
Here on eagles heights,
Knowing Lord Your with us
Sweeping mountain tops,
We fly like eagles Lord
Because You've given us
The spirit in our hearts
To worship more and more.

#68   10-27-98

YOUR GLORY

I really can't describe
The beauty of Your Glory
It's great beyond compare
And awesome on it's own,
There in Your Glory nothing
Hides in You I will abide,
And through Your Glory and
Your Grace of Jesus Christ
Your Son
I'm Yours and Yours alone,
Then someday I'll see
Him face to face and then
I will describe all the
Beauty of
His Glory, that seams to
Overwhelm me now, and
I will tell you how I feel
And then with Him as awesome
As He is the glory of
The Lord
He will shine, yes,
He IS really real.

#69   10-29-98

REVIVAL

Lord we ask You for revival
It starts within our hearts,
Begin in me right here
Please Lord don't delay,
So many others need to know
To You they need draw near,
And give their lives to You
Lord then, to others they
Can show that they have
Given their lives
Revival it will grow,
As we continue in our quest
So others they will know
The saving power of Your love
Oh Lord don't let us go.

Oh Lord send us revival
Go through out the land,
Bring to every city
The message we hold dear,
Fill us with Your presence
And Your Spirit too,
So that we can stand
And know that You are near.

#70   11-17-98

JESUS OUR KING

Jesus came to us as a baby
To live with man here on
Earth, an angle came to Mary
And to her he did say
A child you will give a virgin
Birth, so Mary and Joseph
Were married and off to
Bethlehem they went all of the
Inns they were full there
So a stable became their stay,
King Herold heard of a king
Being born and sent the
Meji's to see he told them,
Bring back information to me,
The Wisemen they gathered
Their gifts to carry, to Jesus
To whom they knew they
Were sent, they came from afar,
And followed the star that lead
Them right there to Jesus,
And when they arrived there
They did find Jesus,
He lay in a manager, and
Thou they found just a baby
A baby that was our King.

#71 11-19-98

TIME

Day is done
And night's begun
And time it's growing
To a close,
Your coming Lord and
We must tell those whose
Hearts are of the world,
They must draw near
To the one whose dear
It's Jesus Christ our King,
We must prepare if
We're going there to our
Heavenly home someday,
So don't set down and
Wear a frown when
You know there's things
To do, you must give
Light with all your might
The Bride Groom is on His way.

#72   1-12-99

LIVING WATER

I stand here in Your presence
Lord and I ask of Thee
To pour the Living Water,
Through me, Lord pour it
Through, so It can flow to
Others who need It just
Like me,
Lord pour out Your Spirit
And keep It flowing through
This life I give to You.
I stand here in Your presence
Asking of You Lord
Asking for the Water
That gives New Life each day,
Lord I am Your vessel
Ready to be used,
So pour through me the
Living Water
So others they might see
The Christ who lives in me.

#73 1-18-99

BESIDE YOU

You cry out for My presence
But I'm only a breath away,
You cry out "Lord please
Touch me" and I'm here
Right by your side,
I'm reaching out to touch you
My child receive Me now
In Me here you can hide,
I hear the songs of Your
Praise to me how they
Do please, I'm reaching out
Please meet My gaze
And take my hands with ease,
I'll take you home,
Here to My Kingdom
Home to be with Me.

#74   1-19-99

LONGING

Capture me my Lord
My soul it longeth after
Thee, rescue me from the
Depths reach through it all,
Way down and pull me up
To solid ground,
Oh Lord my soul is in
Distress I need you
Non the less,
Come rescue me here from
The depths of things I
Can't control,
From the things that only
You and You alone
Can give me peace within,
Oh Lord please come and
Capture me, and make my
Life anew, and keep me
In Your presence
As I worship You,

#75 1-21-99

YOUR LOVE

Your love grows deep within
Me it gives me wings to fly
And oh my spirit it
Flies high,
Your joy it gives me strength
To You I can draw nigh,
My worship takes me higher
The closer I draw to You,
There I soar with wings of
Eagles as high as I can be,
I soar with wings You've
Given me and on those wings
Your there drawing me so high
Up there on eagles wings,
There where I can see
Just how much You've given
You gave Your all for me.

#76 1-29-99

BY YOUR SIDE

My Lord you bend Your
Knee to reach down and
Comfort me so I can climb
Up by Your side and with
You I'll abide, and oh
I take sweet comfort here
Knowing You are near, my
Life I ask for You to
Guide, I know You'll be
Here by my side, I can't
Imagine being on my own and
Walking through things all
Alone, my hand I know that
You will hold as I ask
You Lord my life to mold,
So take me through the
Things where I must go and
Help me learn the things
You want me to know. So with you
Lord I'm here basking in Your
Presence, I rest my head upon
Your side and know that in
You I can hide then You remind
Me I'm Your child and oh my
Heart it wants to dance as I
Look up and meet Your glance.

#77 3-24-99

MOUNTAINS

As my mountains ceased
And my valleys drew still,
My love, for the Lord was
Finally revealed,
As I opened my eyes to
Finally see.
He was standing there
Always waiting for me.
The love that he has shown
Was really quite true.
I couldn't believe that
He lived inside of me
And you! As I opened
The door my life really began.
It's true you know it's
In his own hands.
As He kindly said
I love you so!
My heart and my life I
Placed in His hands!

By Marna Sannes
8-28-98

YOU'RE ALWAYS THERE

You're with me in my pain

You've healed me again
And again. I can feel Your
Love and gentleness
From morning dawn till dusk.
Over me You watch through
The Night 'Till morning
Brings the light
Your hand I know is upon me,
I do believe in Your Grace
And peace, You surround
Me with protection
You've put a hedge,
That's strong and tall
So in my need I know
Where I can call
You'll send Your heavenly
Angels to catch me if I fall
Until the end I can depend
It's You Lord I can call

January 10, 2000

Made in the USA
Columbia, SC
20 May 2023

17017413R00051